SECURITY
COUNTERINTELLIGENCE

OFFICE OF THE NATIONAL COUNTERINTELLIGENCE EXECUTIVE

FOREIGN SPIES STEALING US ECONOMIC SECRETS IN CYBERSPACE

Report to Congress on Foreign Economic Collection and Industrial Espionage, 2009-2011

October 2011

Table of Contents

Annex A

Annex B

List of Text Boxes

List of Charts

Executive Summary

Foreign economic collection and industrial espionage against the United States represent significant and growing threats to the nation's prosperity and security. Cyberspace—where most business activity and development of new ideas now takes place—amplifies these threats by making it possible for malicious actors, whether they are corrupted insiders or foreign intelligence services (FIS), to quickly steal and transfer massive quantities of data while remaining anonymous and hard to detect.

US Technologies and Trade Secrets at Risk in Cyberspace

Foreign collectors of sensitive economic information are able to operate in cyberspace with relatively little risk of detection by their private sector targets. The proliferation of malicious software, prevalence of cyber tool sharing, use of hackers as proxies, and routing of operations through third countries make it difficult to attribute responsibility for computer network intrusions. Cyber tools have enhanced the economic espionage threat, and the Intelligence Community (IC) judges the use of such tools is already a larger threat than more traditional espionage methods.

Economic espionage inflicts costs on companies that range from loss of unique intellectual property to outlays for remediation, but no reliable estimates of the monetary value of these costs exist. Many companies are unaware when their sensitive data is pilfered, and those that find out are often reluctant to report the loss, fearing potential damage to their reputation with investors, customers, and employees. Moreover, victims of trade secret theft use different methods to estimate their losses; some base estimates on the actual costs of developing the stolen information, while others project the loss of future revenues and profits.

Pervasive Threat from Adversaries and Partners

Sensitive US economic information and technology are targeted by the intelligence services, private sector companies, academic and research institutions, and citizens of dozens of countries.

- Chinese actors are the world's most active and persistent perpetrators of economic espionage. US private sector firms and cybersecurity specialists have reported an onslaught of computer network intrusions that have originated in China, but the IC cannot confirm who was responsible.
- Russia's intelligence services are conducting a range of activities to collect economic information and technology from US targets.
- Some US allies and partners use their broad access to US institutions to acquire sensitive US economic and technology information, primarily through aggressive elicitation and other human intelligence (HUMINT) tactics. Some of these states have advanced cyber capabilities.

Outlook

Because the United States is a leader in the development of new technologies and a central player in global financial and trade networks, foreign attempts to collect US technological and economic information will continue at a high level and will represent a growing and persistent threat to US economic security. The nature of the cyber threat will evolve with continuing technological advances in the global information environment.

- Over the next several years, the proliferation of portable devices that connect to the Internet and other networks will continue to create new opportunities for malicious actors to conduct espionage. The trend in both commercial and government organizations toward the pooling of information processing and storage will present even greater challenges to preserving the security and integrity of sensitive information.

- The US workforce will experience a cultural shift that places greater value on access to information and less emphasis on privacy or data protection. At the same time, deepening globalization of economic activities will make national boundaries less of a deterrent to economic espionage than ever.

We judge that the governments of China and Russia will remain aggressive and capable collectors of sensitive US economic information and technologies, particularly in cyberspace.

The relative threat to sensitive US economic information and technologies from a number of countries may change in response to international economic and political developments. One or more fast-growing regional powers may judge that changes in its economic and political interests merit the risk of aggressive cyber and other espionage against US technologies and economic information.

Although foreign collectors will remain interested in all aspects of US economic activity and technology, we judge that the greatest interest may be in the following areas:

- Information and communications technology (ICT), which forms the backbone of nearly every other technology.
- Business information that pertains to supplies of scarce natural resources or that provides foreign actors an edge in negotiations with US businesses or the US Government.
- Military technologies, particularly marine systems, unmanned aerial vehicles (UAVs), and other aerospace/aeronautic technologies.
- Civilian and dual-use technologies in sectors likely to experience fast growth, such as clean energy and health care/pharmaceuticals.

Cyberspace provides relatively small-scale actors an opportunity to become players in economic espionage. Under-resourced governments or corporations could build relationships with hackers to develop customized malware or remote-access exploits to steal sensitive US economic or technology information, just as certain FIS have already done.

- Similarly, political or social activists may use the tools of economic espionage against US companies, agencies, or other entities, with disgruntled insiders leaking information about corporate trade secrets or critical US technology to "hacktivist" groups like WikiLeaks.

Scope Note

This assessment is submitted in compliance with the Intelligence Authorization Act for Fiscal Year 1995, Section 809(b), Public Law 103-359, as amended, which requires that the President biennially submit to Congress updated information on the threat to US industry from foreign economic collection and industrial espionage. This report updates the *14th Annual Report to Congress on Foreign Economic Collection and Industrial Espionage, 2008* and draws primarily on data from 2009-2011.

New Focus and Additional Resources Used for This Year's Report

This report differs from previous editions in three important ways. The first and most significant is the focus. This report gives special attention to foreign collectors' exploitation of cyberspace, while not excluding other established tactics and methods used in foreign economic collection and industrial espionage. This reflects the fact that nearly all business records, research results, and other sensitive economic or technology-related information now exist primarily in digital form. Cyberspace makes it possible for foreign collectors to gather enormous quantities of information quickly and with little risk, whether via remote exploitation of victims' computer networks, downloads of data to external media devices, or e-mail messages transmitting sensitive information.

The second difference from prior reports is that, in addition to researching the large body of intelligence reporting and analysis on economic espionage produced by the Intelligence Community, the Department of Defense (DoD), and other US Government agencies, the drafters of this report consulted new sources of government information.

Third, the Office of the National Counterintelligence Executive (ONCIX) mobilized significant resources from outside the IC during the course of this study. This included outreach to the private sector and, in particular, sponsorship of a conference in November 2010 on cyber-enabled economic espionage at which 26 US Government agencies and 21 private-sector organizations were represented. ONCIX also contracted with outside experts to conduct studies of the academic literature on the cost of economic espionage and the role of the cyber "underground economy."

Definitions of Key Terms

For the purposes of this report, key terms were defined according to both legal and analytic criteria.

The **legal criteria** derive from the language in the Economic Espionage Act (EEA) of 1996 (18 USC §§ 1831-1839). The EAA is concerned in particular with economic espionage and foreign activities to acquire US **trade secrets**. In this context, trade secrets are all forms and types of financial, business, scientific, technical, economic, or engineering information, including patterns, plans, compilations, program devices, formulas, designs, prototypes, methods, techniques, processes, procedures, programs, or codes, whether tangible or intangible, and whether stored or unstored, compiled, or memorialized physically, electronically, graphically, photographically, or in writing, if the owner (the person or entity in whom or in which rightful legal or equitable title to, or license in, is reposed) has taken reasonable measures to keep such information secret and the information derives independent economic value, actual, or potential from not being generally known to, and not being readily ascertainable through, proper means by the public. Activities to acquire these secrets include the following criminal offenses:

- **Economic espionage** occurs when an actor, knowing or intending that his or her actions will benefit any foreign government, instrumentality or agent, knowingly: (1) steals, or without authorization appropriates, carries away, conceals, or obtains by deception or fraud a trade secret; (2) copies, duplicates, reproduces, destroys, uploads, downloads, or transmits that trade secret without authorization; or (3) receives a trade secret knowing that the trade secret had been stolen, appropriated, obtained or converted without authorization (Section 101 of the EEA, 18 USC § 1831).

- **Industrial espionage**, or theft of trade secrets, occurs when an actor, intending or knowing that his or her offense will injure the owner of a trade secret of a product produced for or placed in interstate or foreign commerce, acts with the intent to convert that trade secret to the economic benefit of anyone other than the owner by: (1) stealing, or without authorization appropriating, carrying away, concealing, or obtaining by deception or fraud information related to that secret; (2) copying, duplicating, reproducing, destroying, uploading, downloading, or otherwise transmiting that information without authorization; or (3) receiving that information knowing that that information had been stolen, appropriated, obtained or converted without authorization (Section 101 of the EEA, 18 USC § 1832).

The following definitions reflect the experience of IC cyber, counterintelligence, and economic analysts:

- **Cyberspace** is the interdependent network of information technology (IT) infrastructures, and includes the Internet, telecommunications networks, computer systems, and embedded processors and controllers in critical industries.
- **Sensitive** is defined as information or technology (a) that has been classified or controlled by a US Government organization or restricted in a proprietary manner by a US corporation or other institution, or (b) that has or may reasonably be expected to have military, intelligence, or other uses with implications for US national security, or (c) that may enhance the economic competitiveness of US firms in global markets.

Contributors

ONCIX compiled this report using inputs and reporting from many US Government agencies and departments, including the Air Force Office of Special Investigations (AFOSI), Army Counterintelligence Center (ACIC), Central Intelligence Agency (CIA), Defense Intelligence Agency (DIA), Defense Security Service (DSS), Department of Energy (DoE), Department of Health and Human Services (HHS), Department of State (DoS), Federal Bureau of Investigation (FBI), National Geospatial-Intelligence Agency (NGA), National Reconnaissance Office (NRO), National Security Agency (NSA), and Naval Criminal Investigative Service (NCIS).

Foreign Spies Stealing US Economic Secrets in Cyberspace

US Technologies and Trade Secrets at Risk in Cyberspace

The pace of foreign economic collection and industrial espionage activities against major US corporations and US Government agencies is accelerating. FIS, corporations, and private individuals increased their efforts in 2009-2011 to steal proprietary technologies, which cost millions of dollars to develop and represented tens or hundreds of millions of dollars in potential profits. The computer networks of a broad array of US Government agencies, private companies, universities, and other institutions—all holding large volumes of sensitive economic information—were targeted by cyber espionage; much of this activity appears to have originated in China.

Increasingly, economic collection and industrial espionage occur in cyberspace, reflecting dramatic technological, economic, and social changes that have taken place in recent years in the ways that economic, scientific, and other sensitive information is created, used, and stored. Today, nearly all business records, research results, and other sensitive economic data are digitized and accessible on networks worldwide. Cyber collection can take many forms, including: simple visits to a US company's website for the collection of openly available information; a corporate insider's downloading of proprietary information onto a thumb drive at the behest of a foreign rival; or intrusions launched by FIS or other actors against the computer networks of a private company, federal agency, or an individual.

The Appeal of Collecting in Cyberspace

Cyberspace is a unique complement to the espionage environment because it provides foreign collectors with relative anonymity, facilitates the transfer of a vast amount of information, and makes it more difficult for victims and governments to assign blame by masking geographic locations.

Security and attribution. Collectors operating in a cyber environment can collect economic information with less risk of detection. This is particularly true for remote computer network exploitation (CNE). Foreign collectors take advantage of the fact that it is difficult to detect and to attribute responsibility for these operations.

There is increasing similarity between the tools, tactics, and techniques used by various actors, which reduces the reliability of using these factors to identify those responsible for computer network intrusions.

- The proliferation of malicious software (malware) presents opportunities for intelligence services and other actors to launch operations with limited resources and without developing unique tools that can be associated with them.

- Hacker websites are prevalent across the Internet, and tool sharing is common, causing intrusions by unrelated actors to exhibit similar technical characteristics.

- FIS and other foreign entities have used independent hackers at times to augment their capabilities and act as proxies for intrusions, thereby providing plausible deniability.

- Many actors route operations through computers in third countries or physically operate from third countries to obscure the origin of their activity.

Another factor adding to the challenge of attribution is the diverging perspectives of the actual targets of economic espionage in cyberspace.

- At a conference sponsored by ONCIX in November 2010, US private industry representatives said they saw little difference between cybercrime—for example, identity theft or the misappropriation of intellectual property such as the counterfeiting of commercial video or audio recordings—and the collection of economic or technology information by intelligence services or other foreign entities. Private sector organizations are often less concerned with attribution and focus instead on damage control and prevention; moreover, few companies have the ability to identify cyber intruders.

- US Government law enforcement and intelligence agencies, on the other hand, seek to establish attribution as part of their mission to counter FIS and other clandestine information collectors. They, unlike companies, also have the intelligence collection authorities and capabilities needed to break multiple layers of cover and to establish attribution where possible.

Cyberspace also offers greater security to the perpetrator in cases involving insiders. Although audits or similar cyber security measures may flag illicit information downloads from a corporate network, a malicious actor can quickly and safely transfer a data set once it is copied. A physical meeting is unnecessary between the corrupted insider and the persons or organizations the information is being collected for, reducing the risk of detection.

Faster and cheaper. Cyberspace makes possible the near instantaneous transfer of enormous quantities of economic and other information. Until fairly recently, economic espionage often required that insiders pass large volumes of documents to their handlers in physical form—a lengthy process of collection, collation, transportation, and exploitation.

- Dongfan Chung was an engineer with Rockwell and Boeing who worked on the B-1 bomber, space shuttle, and other projects and was sentenced in early 2010 to 15 years in prison for economic espionage on behalf of the Chinese aviation industry. At the time of his arrest, 250,000 pages of sensitive documents were found in his house. This is suggestive of the volume of information Chung could have passed to his handlers between 1979 and 2006.[a] The logistics of handling the physical volume of these documents—which would fill nearly four 4-drawer filing cabinets— would have required considerable attention from Chung and his handlers. With current technology, all the data in the documents hidden in Chung's house would fit onto one inexpensive CD.[b]

[a]Chung was prosecuted only for possession of these documents with the intent to benefit the People's Republic of China (PRC) and acting as an unregistered foreign agent for China. He was not charged with communication of this information to the PRC or any other foreign entity.

[b]On average, one page of typed text holds 2 kilobytes (KB) of data; thus, 250,000 pages x 2 KB/page = 500,000 KB, or 488 megabytes (MB). A data CD with a capacity of 700 MB retails for $0.75, and a flashdrive with a capacity of 4 gigabytes costs about $13.00.

Extra-territoriality. In addition to the problem of attribution, it often is difficult to establish the geographic location of an act of economic espionage that takes place in cyberspace. Uncertainty about the physical location of the act provides cover for the perpetrators and complicates efforts by US Government law enforcement or intelligence agencies to respond.

Non-Cyber Methods of Economic Espionage

Although this assessment focuses on the use of cyber tools and the cyber environment in foreign efforts to collect sensitive US economic information and technologies, a variety of other methods also remain in use.

***Requests for Information (RFI).** Foreign collectors make unsolicited direct and indirect requests for information via personal contacts, telephone, e-mail, fax, and other forms of communication and often seek classified, sensitive, or export-controlled information.*

***Solicitation or Marketing of Services.** Foreign companies seek entrée into US firms and other targeted institutions by pursuing business relationships that provide access to sensitive or classified information, technologies, or projects.*

***Conferences, Conventions, and Trade Shows.** These public venues offer opportunities for foreign adversaries to gain access to US information and experts in dual-use and sensitive technologies.*

***Official Foreign Visitors and Exploitation of Joint Research.** Foreign government organizations, including intelligence services, use official visits to US Government and cleared defense contractor facilities, as well as joint research projects between foreign and US entities, to target and collect information.*

***Foreign Targeting of US Visitors Overseas.** Whether traveling for business or personal reasons, US travelers overseas—businesspeople, US Government employees, and contractors—are routinely targeted by foreign collectors, especially if they are assessed* *as having access to some sensitive information. Some US allies engage in this practice, as do less friendly powers such as Russia and China. Targeting takes many forms: exploitation of electronic media and devices, surreptitious entry into hotel rooms, aggressive surveillance, and attempts to set up sexual or romantic entanglements.*

Open Source Information. *Foreign collectors are aware that much US economic and technological information is available in professional journals, social networking and other public websites, and the media.*

Large but Uncertain Costs

Losses of sensitive economic information and technologies to foreign entities represent significant costs to US national security. The illicit transfer of technology with military applications to a hostile state such as Iran or North Korea could endanger the lives of US and allied military personnel. The collection of confidential US Government economic information—whether by a potential adversary or a current ally—could undercut US ability to develop and enact policies in areas ranging from climate change negotiations to reform of financial market regulations. The theft of trade secrets from US companies by foreign economic rivals undermines the corporate sector's ability to create jobs, generate revenues, foster innovation, and lay the economic foundation for prosperity and national security.

Data on the effects of the theft of trade secrets and other sensitive information are incomplete, however, according to an ONCIX-sponsored survey of academic literature on the costs of economic espionage.

- Many victims of economic espionage are unaware of the crime until years after loss of the information.

- Even when a company knows its sensitive information has been stolen by an insider or that its computer networks have been penetrated, it may choose not to report the event to the FBI or other law enforcement agencies. No

legal requirement to report a loss of sensitive information or a remote computer intrusion exists, and announcing a security breach of this kind could tarnish a company's reputation and endanger its relationships with investors, bankers, suppliers, customers, and other stakeholders.

- A company also may not want to publicly accuse a corporate rival or foreign government of stealing its secrets from fear of offending potential customers or business partners.

- Finally, it is inherently difficult to assign an economic value to some types of information that are subject to theft. It would, for example, be nearly impossible to estimate the monetary value of talking points for a meeting between officials from a US company and foreign counterparts.

The Cost of Economic Espionage to One Company

Data exist in some specific cases on the damage that economic espionage or theft of trade secrets has inflicted on individual companies. For example, an employee of Valspar Corporation unlawfully downloaded proprietary paint formulas valued at $20 million, which he intended to take to a new job in China, according to press reports. This theft represented about one-eighth of Valspar's reported profits in 2009, the year the employee was arrested.

Even in those cases where a company recognizes it has been victimized by economic espionage and reports the incident, calculation of losses is challenging and can produce ambiguous results. Different methods can be used that yield divergent estimates, which adds to the difficulty of meaningfully comparing cases or aggregating estimated losses.

- An executive from a major industrial company told ONCIX representatives in late 2010 that his company has used historical costs—tallying salaries, supplies, utilities, and similar direct expenses—to estimate losses from cases of attempted theft of its trade secrets. This method has the advantage of using known and objective data, but it underestimates the extent of losses in many cases because it does not capture the effect of lost intellectual property on future sales and profits.

- Harm is calculated in US civil court cases involving the theft of trade secrets by measuring the "lost profits" or "reasonable royalty" that a company is unable to earn because of the theft. Although this method requires subjective assumptions about market share, profitability, and similar factors, it does offer a more complete calculation of the cost than relying strictly on historical accounting data.

- Estimates from academic literature on the losses from economic espionage range so widely as to be meaningless—from $2 billion to $400 billion or more a year—reflecting the scarcity of data and the variety of methods used to calculate losses.

A Possible Proxy Measure of the Costs of Economic Espionage to the United States

New ideas are often a company's or an agency's most valuable information and are usually of greatest interest to foreign collectors. Corporate and government spending on research and development (R&D) is one measure of the cost of developing new ideas, and hence is an indicator of the value of the information that is most vulnerable to economic espionage. R&D spending has been tracked by the National Science Foundation (NSF) since 1953. For 2008, the most recent year available, the NSF

calculated that US industry, the Federal Government, universities, and other nonprofit organizations expended $398 billion on R&D, or 2.8 percent of the US Gross Domestic Product.

Pervasive Threat from Intelligence Adversaries and Partners

Many states view economic espionage as an essential tool in achieving national security and economic prosperity. Their economic espionage programs combine collection of open source information, HUMINT, signals intelligence (SIGINT), and cyber operations—to include computer network intrusions and exploitation of insider access to corporate and proprietary networks—to develop information that could give these states a competitive edge over the United States and other rivals.

- China and Russia view themselves as strategic competitors of the United States and are the most aggressive collectors of US economic information and technology.

- Other countries with closer ties to the United States have conducted CNE and other forms of intelligence collection to obtain US economic and technology data, often taking advantage of the access they enjoy as allies or partners to collect sensitive military data and information on other programs.

Recent Insider Thefts of Corporate Trade Secrets with a Link to China

David Yen Lee…chemist with Valspar Corporation…between late 2008 and early 2009 used access to internal computer network to download about 160 secret formulas for paints and coatings to his own storage media…intended to take this proprietary information to a new job with Nippon Paint in Shanghai, China…arrested March 2009…pleaded guilty to one count of theft of trade secrets; sentenced in December 2010 to 15 months in prison.

Meng Hong…DuPont Corporation research chemist…in mid-2009 downloaded proprietary information on organic light-emitting diodes (OLED) to personal e-mail account and thumb drive…intended to transfer this information to Peking University, where he had accepted a faculty position; sought Chinese Government funding to commercialize OLED research…arrested October 2009…pleaded guilty to one count of theft of trade secrets; sentenced in October 2010 to 14 months in prison.

Yu Xiang Dong (aka Mike Yu)…product engineer with Ford Motor Company who in December 2006 accepted a job at Ford's China branch…copied approximately 4,000 Ford documents onto an external hard drive to help obtain a job with a Chinese automotive company…arrested in October 2009…pleaded guilty to two counts of theft of trade secrets; sentenced in April 2011 to 70 months in prison.

China: Persistent Collector

Chinese leaders consider the first two decades of the 21st century to be a window of strategic opportunity for their country to focus on economic growth, independent innovation, scientific and technical advancement, and growth of the renewable energy sector.

China's intelligence services, as well as private companies and other entities, frequently seek to exploit Chinese citizens or persons with family ties to China who can use their insider access to corporate networks to steal trade secrets using removable media devices or e-mail. Of the seven cases that were adjudicated under the Economic Espionage Act—both Title 18 USC § 1831 and § 1832—in Fiscal Year 2010, six involved a link to China.

US corporations and cyber security specialists also have reported an onslaught of computer network intrusions originating from Internet Protocol (IP) addresses in China, which private sector specialists call "advanced persistent threats." Some of these reports have alleged a Chinese corporate or government sponsor of the activity, but the IC has not been able to attribute many of these private sector data breaches to a state sponsor. Attribution is especially difficult when the event occurs weeks or months before the victims request IC or law enforcement help.

- In a February 2011 study, McAfee attributed an intrusion set they labeled "Night Dragon" to an IP address located in China and indicated the intruders had exfiltrated data from the computer systems of global oil, energy, and petrochemical companies. Starting in November 2009, employees of targeted companies were subjected to social engineering, spear-phishing e-mails, and network exploitation. The goal of the intrusions was to obtain information on sensitive competitive proprietary operations and on financing of oil and gas field bids and operations.

- In January 2010, VeriSign iDefense identified the Chinese Government as the sponsor of intrusions into Google's networks. Google subsequently made accusations that its source code had been taken—a charge that Beijing continues to deny.

- Mandiant reported in 2010 that information was pilfered from the corporate networks of a US Fortune 500 manufacturing company during business negotiations in which that company was looking to acquire a Chinese firm. Mandiant's report indicated that the US manufacturing company lost sensitive data on a weekly basis and that this may have helped the Chinese firm attain a better negotiating and pricing position.

- Participants at an ONCIX conference in November 2010 from a range of US private sector industries reported that client lists, merger and acquisition data, company information on pricing, and financial data were being extracted from company networks—especially those doing business with China.

Russia: Extensive, Sophisticated Operations

Motivated by Russia's high dependence on natural resources, the need to diversify its economy, and the belief that the global economic system is tilted toward US and other Western interests at the expense of Russia, Moscow's highly capable intelligence services are using HUMINT, cyber, and other operations to collect economic information and technology to support Russia's economic development and security.

- For example, the 10 Russian Foreign Intelligence Service (SVR) "illegals" arrested in June 2010 were tasked to collect economic and technology information, highlighting the importance of these issues to Moscow.[c]

[c]An illegal is an officer or employee of an intelligence organization who is dispatched abroad and who has no overt connection with the intelligence organization with which he or she is connected or with the government operating that intelligence organization.

Russian Leaders Link Intelligence Operations and Economic Interests

The SVR *"must be able to swiftly and adequately evaluate changes in the international economic situation, understand the consequences for the domestic economy and…more actively protect the economic interests of our companies abroad."*
—Vladimir Putin, President, Russian Federation, October 2007

"Intelligence…aims at supporting the process of modernization of our country and creating the optimal conditions for the development of its science and technology."
—Mikhail Fradkov, Director, SVR, December 2010

Source: Russian press reports.

US Partners: Leveraging Access

Certain allies and other countries that enjoy broad access to US Government agencies and the private sector conduct economic espionage to acquire sensitive US information and technologies. Some of these states have advanced cyber capabilities.

Outlook

Because the United States is a leader in the development of new technologies and a central player in global financial and trade networks, foreign attempts to collect US technological and economic information will remain at high levels and continue to threaten US economic security. The nature of these attempts will be shaped by the accelerating evolution of cyberspace, policy choices made by the economic and political rivals of the United States, and broad economic and technological developments.

Near Certainties

Evolving cyber environment. Over the next three to five years, we expect that four broad factors will accelerate the rate of change in information technology and communications technology in ways that are likely to disrupt security procedures and provide new openings for collection of sensitive US economic and technology information. These were identified in studies conducted by Cisco Systems and discussed at the ONCIX conference in November 2010. At the same time, the growing complexity and density of cyberspace will provide more cover for remote cyber intruders and make it even harder than today to establish attribution for these incidents.

The first factor is a *technological shift*. According to a Cisco Systems study, the number of devices such as smartphones and laptops in operation worldwide that can connect to the Internet and other networks is expected to increase from about 12.5 billion in 2010 to 25 billion in 2015. This will cause a proliferation in the number of operating systems and endpoints that malicious actors such as foreign intelligence services or corrupt insiders can exploit to obtain sensitive information. Meanwhile, the underlying hardware and software of information systems will become more complex.

- Marketing and revenue imperatives will continue to lead IT product vendors to release products with less than exhaustive testing, which will also create opportunities for remote exploitation.

An *economic shift* will change the way that corporations, government agencies, and other organizations share storage, computing, network, and application resources. The move to a "cloud computing" paradigm—which is much cheaper for companies than hosting computer services in-

Projected Growth in Number of IT Devices Connected to Networks and the Internet, 2003-2020

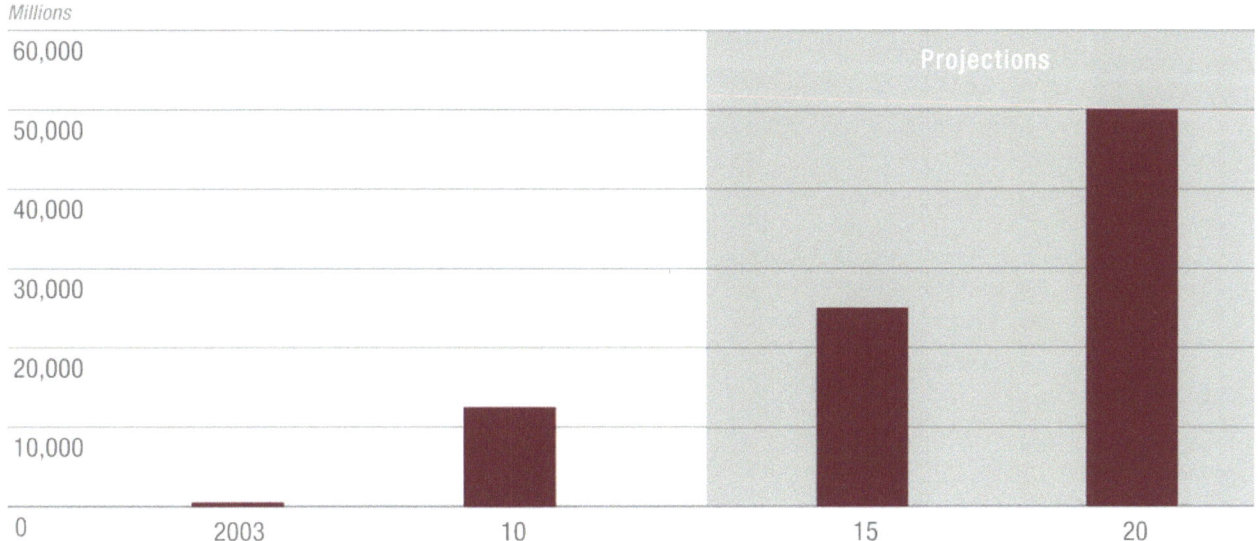

Millions

Projections

Source: CISCO Systems

house—will mean that employees will be able to work and access data anywhere and at any time, and not just while they are at the office, laboratory, or factory. Although cloud computing offers some security advantages, such as robust backup in the event of a systems disruption, the movement of data among multiple locations will increase the opportunities for theft or manipulation by malicious actors.

The *cultural shift* involves the rise in the US work-force of different expectations regarding work, privacy, and collaboration. Workers will tend to draw few distinctions between their home and work lives, and they will expect free access to any information they want—whether personal or professional—from any location.

- Current technology already enables many US workers to conduct business from remote locations and on-the-go at any time of day. This alteration relies on the ability of workers to connect to one another and their companies through the Internet—increasing their flexibility and corporate productivity but potentially increasing the risk of theft.

Finally, a *geopolitical shift* will continue the globalization of economic activities and knowledge creation. National boundaries will deter economic espionage less than ever as more business is conducted from wherever workers can access the Internet. The globalization of the supply chain for new—and increasingly interconnected—IT products will offer more opportunities for malicious actors to compromise the integrity and security of these devices.

Little change in principal threats. The IC anticipates that China and Russia will remain aggressive and capable collectors of sensitive US economic information and technologies, particularly in cyberspace. Both will almost certainly continue to deploy significant resources and a wide array of tactics to acquire this information from US sources, motivated by the desire to achieve economic, strategic, and military parity with the United States.

China will continue to be driven by its longstanding policy of "catching up fast and surpassing" Western powers. An emblematic program in this drive is Project 863, which provides funding and guidance for efforts to clandestinely acquire US technology and sensitive economic information. The project was launched in 1986 to enhance China's economic competitiveness and narrow the science and technology gap between China and the West in areas such as nanotechnology, computers, and biotechnology.

- The growing interrelationships between Chinese and US companies—such as the employment of Chinese-national technical experts at US facilities and the off-shoring of US production and R&D to facilities in China—will offer Chinese Government agencies and businesses increasing opportunities to collect sensitive US economic information.

- Chinese actors will continue conducting CNE against US targets.

Two trends may increase the threat from Russian collection against US economic information and technology over the next several years.

- The many Russian immigrants with advanced technical skills who work for leading US companies may be increasingly targeted for recruitment by the Russian intelligence services.

- Russia's increasing economic integration with the West is likely to lead to a greater number of Russian companies affiliated with the intelligence services—often through their employment of ostensibly retired intelligence officers—doing business in the United States.

Technologies likely to be of greatest interest. Although all aspects of US economic activity and technology are of potential interest to foreign intelligence collectors, we judge that the highest interest may be in the following areas.

Information and communications technology (ICT). ICT is a sector likely to remain one of the highest priorities of foreign collectors. The computerization of manufacturing and the push for connectedness mean that ICT forms the backbone of nearly every other technology used in both civilian and military applications.

- Beijing's Project 863, for example, lists the development of "key technologies for the construction of China's information infrastructure" as the first of four priorities.

Military technologies. We expect foreign entities will continue efforts to collect information on the full array of US military technologies in use or under development. Two areas are likely to be of particular interest:

- *Marine systems.* China's desire to jump-start development of a blue-water navy—to project power in the Taiwan Strait and defend maritime trade routes—will drive efforts to obtain sensitive US marine systems technologies.

- *Aerospace/aeronautics.* The air supremacy demonstrated by US military operations in recent decades will remain a driver of foreign efforts to collect US aerospace and aeronautics technologies. The greatest interest may be in UAVs because of their recent successful use for both intelligence gathering and kinetic operations in Afghanistan, Iraq, and elsewhere.

Civilian and dual-use technologies. We expect that foreign collection on US civilian and dual-use technologies will follow overall patterns of investment and trade. The following sectors—which are expected to experience surges in investment and are priorities for China—may be targeted more aggressively.

- *Clean technologies.* Energy-generating technologies that produce reduced carbon dioxide and other emissions will be the fastest growing investment sectors in nine of 11 countries recently surveyed by a US consulting company—a survey that included China, France, and India.

- *Advanced materials and manufacturing techniques.* One focus of China's 863 program is achieving mastery of key new materials and advanced manufacturing technologies to boost industrial competitiveness, particularly in the aviation and high-speed rail sectors. Russia and Iran have aggressive programs for developing and collecting on one specific area of advanced materials development: nanotechnology.

Rising Prices Increase Value of Commodity Information to Foreign Collectors (Index, 2002=100)

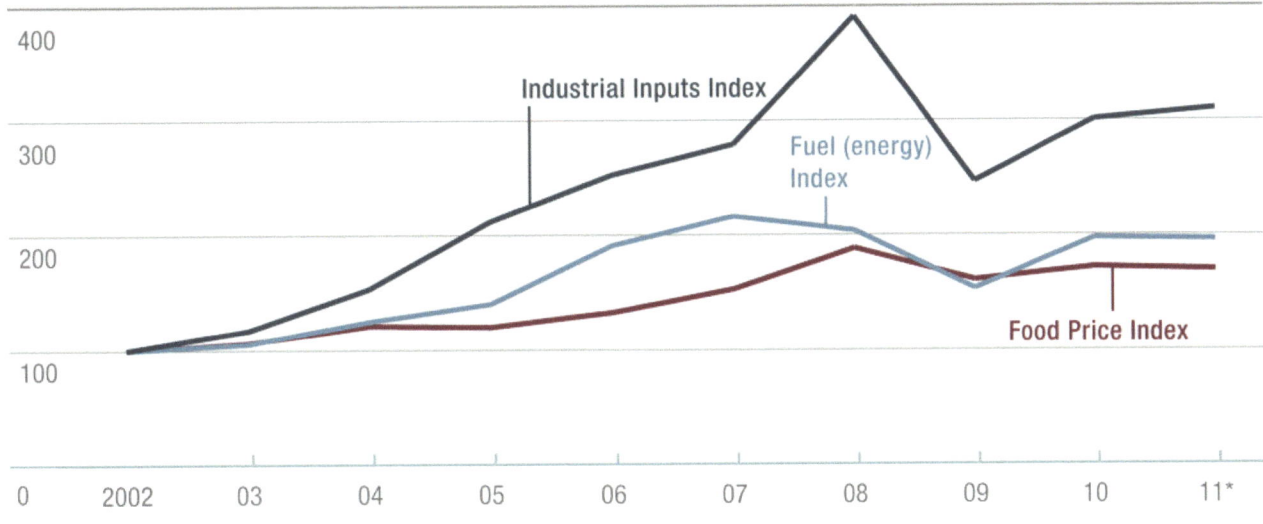

*2011 values as of April.

Source: International Monetary Fund, World Economic Outlook Database.

- *Healthcare, pharmaceuticals, and related technologies.* Healthcare services and medical devices/equipment will be two of the five fastest growing international investment sectors, according to a US consulting firm. The massive R&D costs for new products in these sectors—up to $1 billion for a single drug—the possibility of earning monopoly profits from a popular new pharmaceutical, and the growing need for medical care by aging populations in China, Russia, and elsewhere are likely to drive interest in collecting valuable US healthcare, pharmaceutical, and related information.

- *Agricultural technology.* Surging prices for food—which have increased by 70 percent since 2002, according to the food price index published by the International Monetary Fund (IMF)—and for other agricultural products may increase the value of and interest in collecting on US technologies related to crop production, such as genetic engineering, improved seeds, and fertilizer.[d]

Business information. As with technologies, we assess that nearly all categories of sensitive US economic information will be targeted by foreign entities, but the following sectors may be of greatest interest:

Energy and other natural resources. Surging prices for energy and industrial commodities—which have increased by 210 percent and 96 percent, respectively, since 2002 according to IMF indices—may make US company information on these resources priority targets for intelligence services and other collectors.[e]

- As noted earlier, cyber intrusions originating in China, but not necessarily attributed to the Chinese Government, since at least 2009 have targeted sensitive operational and project-financing information of US and other international oil, energy, and petrochemical companies, according to reports published by McAfee.

[d]The IMF's Food Price Index is a weighted index that includes the spot prices of cereal grains, vegetable oils and protein meals, meat, seafood, sugar, bananas, and oranges.

[e]The Fuel (energy) index published by the IMF is a weighted index that includes the spot prices of crude oil, natural gas, and coal. The Industrial Inputs Index is a weighted index that includes the spot price of agricultural raw materials (timber, fibers, rubber and hides) and non-precious metals (such as copper, aluminum, and iron ore).

Business deals. Some foreign companies—at times helped by their home countries' intelligence services—will collect sensitive information from US economic actors that are negotiating contracts with or competing against them.

Macroeconomic information. In the wake of the global financial crisis of 2008-2009 and related volatility in the values of currencies and commodities, sensitive macroeconomic information held by the US private sector and government agencies is likely to remain a prime collection target for both intelligence services and foreign corporations. Chinese and Russian intelligence collectors may pursue, for example, non-public data on topics such as interest rate policy to support their policymakers' efforts to advance the role of their currencies and displace the dollar in international trade and finance. Such information also could help boost the performance of sovereign wealth funds controlled by governments like China's, whose China Investment Corporation managed more than $300 billion in investments as of late 2010.[f]

Possible Game Changers

Any of a range of less-likely developments over the next several years could increase the threat from economic espionage against US interests.

Emergence of new state threats. The relative threat to sensitive US economic information and technologies from different countries is likely to evolve as a function of international economic and political developments.

One or more fast-growing regional powers may judge that changes in its economic and political interests merit the risk of an aggressive program of espionage against US technologies and sensitive economic information.

Growing role of non-state and non-corporate actors. The migration of most business and technology development activities to cyberspace is making it easier for actors without the resources of a nation-state or a large corporation to become players in economic espionage. Such new actors may act as surrogates or contractors for intelligence services or major companies, or they could conduct espionage against sensitive US economic information and technology in pursuit of their own objectives.

Hackers for hire. Some intelligence services with less-developed cyber programs already use relationships with nominally independent hackers to augment their capabilities to target political and military information or to carry out operations against regime enemies. For example, the Iranian Cyber Army, a hacker group with links to the Iranian Government, has used social engineering techniques to obtain control over Internet domains and disrupt the political opposition, according to research conducted under an ONCIX contract.

No evidence of involvement by independent hackers in economic espionage has been found in intelligence or academic reporting to date, in large part due to the absence of a profitable market for the resale of stolen information. This "cyber underground" could, however, become a fruitful recruiting ground for the tools and talents needed to support economic espionage. Following the model used by some intelligence services in exploiting the cyber environment for political or military espionage, a foreign government or corporation could build relationships with hackers for the development of customized malware or remote access exploits for the exfiltration of sensitive US economic or technology information.

Hacktivists. Political or social activists also may use the tools of economic espionage against US companies, agencies, or other entities. The self-styled whistleblowing group WikiLeaks has already published computer files provided by corporate insiders indicating allegedly illegal or unethical behavior at a Swiss bank, a Netherlands-based commodities company, and an international pharmaceutical trade association. LulzSec—another hacktivist group—has exfiltrated data from several businesses that it posted for public viewing on its website.

---

[f] A sovereign wealth fund is a government investment fund, funded by foreign currency reserves but managed separately from official currency reserves. In other words, it is a pool of money that a government invests for profit.

Corporate trade secrets or information about critical US technology may be at similar risk of disclosure to activist groups by disgruntled insiders.

- Antipoverty activists, for instance, could seek to publish the details of a new medicine under development by a US pharmaceutical company, with the goal of ending the firm's "monopoly" profits and making the product more widely available.
- Antiwar groups could disclose information about a new weapons system in the hope of dissuading the United States from deploying it.

Page left intentionally blank

Annex A

Intelligence Community and Private Sector Measures to Counter Economic Espionage and Manage Collection in Cyberspace

The IC is working closely with all segments of the public and private sectors to try to counter espionage activities that target our sensitive economic data and technology. We cannot expect to stop entirely or prevent hostile activity to collect US public and private sector information, but we can work to minimize the activity and mitigate its effects.

Intelligence Community Responses

The IC and especially counterintelligence (CI) officers have already taken a number of steps to improve collaboration, collection, and analysis across the CI, economics, and cyber disciplines.

Improved collaboration. Over the past few years, the IC has established multiple organizations and working groups to better understand the cyber espionage threat. These have contributed to a better understanding of the use of cyber in economic espionage.

- The National Cyber Counterintelligence Working Group established in 2011 is composed of 16 IC and other federal agencies and is creating a coordinated response to the cyber intelligence threat.
- The FBI is leading the National Cyber Investigative Joint Task Force, which brings together multiple agencies to collaborate on intrusions into US systems.

CI officers are considering an expansion of collaboration to include enhanced information sharing with Department of Justice attorneys. CI officers could introduce questions for attorneys to pose to offenders during the investigation process. They might also look at ways to tie plea bargains and sentencing decisions to suspects' willingness to cooperate with the CI Community during damage assessments.

Improved analysis and collection. The IC has made great strides over the past few years in understanding the cyber espionage threat to US Government systems, but our knowledge of cyber-enabled economic espionage threats to the US private sector remains limited.

Defense Model Shows Limits to Mandatory Reporting Requirements

DoD's partnership with cleared defense contractors (CDCs) highlights difficulties in establishing an effective framework to improve the IC's understanding of foreign cyber threats and promote threat awareness in industry. The defense industrial base conducts $400 billion in business with the Pentagon each year and maintains a growing repository of government information and intellectual property on unclassified networks. CDCs are required to file reports of suspicious contacts indicative of foreign threats—including cyber—to their personnel, information, and technologies.

- *Despite stringent reporting requirements for CDCs, DSS reports that only 10 percent of CDCs actually provide any sort of reporting in a given year.*
- *Another shortcoming of the defense model is that contractors do not always report theft of intellectual property unless it relates specifically to Pentagon contracts, according to outreach discussions with corporate officers.*
- *Corporate security officers also have noted that US Government reporting procedures are often cumbersome and redundant, with military services and agencies such as DSS and the FBI often seeking the same information but in different formats.*

Operations. CI professionals are adapting how they detect, deter, and disrupt collection activity in cyberspace because of the challenges in detecting the traditional indicators of collection activity—spotting, assessing, and recruiting.

It is imperative that we improve our ability to attribute technical and human activity in the cyber environment so that we can improve our understanding of the threat and our ability to generate a greater number of offensive CI responses.

Training and awareness. Expanding our national education and awareness campaign aimed at individuals and corporations is an essential defensive strategy for countering threats from cyber-enabled economic collection and espionage. We are building on current outreach initiatives that the FBI and ONCIX have already initiated.

- IC outreach to all US Government agencies, state and local governments, academia, nongovernmental organizations, industry associations, and companies is critical for promoting threat awareness, as well as for a better understanding of nongovernmental perspectives. Partners outside the IC are becoming aware of the wide range of potentially sensitive information in their possession and the extent of foreign efforts to acquire it.

- Outreach efforts include awareness and mitigation strategies for insider threat issues. The unique access of insiders to information technology systems and organizational processes makes this the most dangerous approach to cyber economic collection and espionage, as insiders can act alone to guide CNE or to download sensitive data to portable media.

ONCIX already engages in dialogue with ASIS International—an industry association for security professionals—and the Department of State's Overseas Security Advisory Council on the challenges facing both the public and private sectors with regard to cyber-enabled economic collection and espionage.

Finally, IC outreach efforts to the private sector on economic espionage need to fully engage corporate and other partners in order to be credible. We can facilitate partnerships to share best practices, threat updates and analysis, and data on intrusions. One company security officer has suggested that

the IC must speak to industry in language geared to the private sector's needs and experience and emphasize, for example, that the protection of trade secrets is critical to corporate profitability and growth.

As a follow-up to the public/private sector Workshop on Cyber-Enabled Economic Espionage held in 2010, ONCIX should consider sponsoring another conference with Department of Justice and private sector stakeholders on lessons learned regarding successful convictions under Section 1831 of the Economic Espionage Act.

Corporate Responses

The private sector already has a fiduciary duty to account for corporate risk and the bottom-line effects of data breaches, economic espionage, and loss or degradation of services. A key responsibility of chief executive officers and boards of directors is to ensure that the protection of trade secrets and computer networks is an integral part of all corporate decisions and processes and that all managers—not just security and information systems officials—have a stake in the outcome.[a] Viewing network security and data protection as a business matter that has a significant impact on profitability will lead to more effective risk management and ensure that adequate resources are allocated to address cyber threats to companies.

- Only 5 percent of corporate chief financial officers are involved in network security matters, and just 13 percent of companies have a cross-functional cyber risk team that bridges the technical, financial, and other elements of a company, according to a 2010 study.

Judicial Mandate for Boards of Directors To Secure Corporate Information

Delaware's Court of Chancery ruled in the 1996 Caremark case that a director's good faith duty includes a duty to attempt to ensure that a corporate

---

[a]Legal and human resources officers are two sets of key stakeholders given the role that corporate insiders have historically played in contributing to economic espionage and the theft of trade secrets.

information and reporting system exists and that failure to do so may render a director liable for losses caused by the illegal conduct of employees. The Delaware Supreme Court clarified this language in the 2006 Stone v. Ritter *case—deciding that directors may be liable for the damages resulting from legal violations committed by the employees of a corporation, if directors fail to implement a reporting system or controls or fail to monitor such systems.*

Companies that successfully manage the economic espionage threat realize and convey to their employees that threats to corporate data extend beyond company firewalls to include other locations where company data is moved or stored. These include cloud sites, home computers, laptops, portable electronic devices, portable data assistants, and social networking sites.

- A survey of 200 information technology and security professionals in February 2011 revealed that 65 percent do not know what files and data leave their enterprise.

- According to a March 2011 press report, 57 percent of employees save work files to external devices on a weekly basis.

- E-mail systems are often less protected than databases yet contain vast quantities of stored data. E-mail remains one of the quickest and easiest ways for individuals to collaborate—and for intruders to enter a company's network and steal data.

Cyber threats to company information are compounded when employees access data through portable devices or network connections while traveling overseas. Many FIS co-opt hotel staffs to allow access to portable devices left unattended in rooms. It is also much easier for FIS to monitor and exploit network connections within their own borders.

- Foreign collectors engage in virtual methods to collect sensitive corporate data and take advantage of victims' reluctance to report digital penetrations and low awareness of foreign targeting, according to legal academic research.

Corporate security officers have told ONCIX that US Government reporting procedures on economic espionage and cyber intrusions are often cumbersome and redundant. Agencies such as DSS and the FBI often seek the same information but in different formats.

Best Practices in Data Protection Strategies and Due Diligence for Corporations

Information Strategy

- Develop a "transparency strategy" that determines how closed or open the company needs to be based on the services provided.

Insider Threat Programs and Awareness

- Institute security training and awareness campaigns; convey threats to company information accessed through portable devices and when traveling abroad.

- Establish an insider threat program that consists of information technology-enabled threat detection, foreign travel and contact notifications, personnel security and evaluation, insider threat awareness and training, and reporting and analysis.

- Conduct background checks that vet users before providing them company information.

- Implement non-disclosure agreements with employees and business partners.

- Establish employee exit procedures; most employees who steal intellectual property commit the theft within one month of resignation.

Effective Data Management

- Get a handle on company data—not just in databases but also in e-mail messages, on individual computers, and as data objects in web portals; categorize and classify the data, and choose the most appropriate set of controls and markings for each class of data; identify which data should be kept and for how long. Understand that it is impossible to protect everything.

- Establish compartmentalized access programs to protect unique trade secrets and proprietary information; centralize intellectual property data—which will make for better security and facilitate information sharing.

- Restrict distribution of sensitive data; establish a shared data infrastructure to reduce the quantity of data held by the organization and discourage unnecessary printing and reproduction.

Network Security, Auditing, and Monitoring

- Conduct real-time monitoring/auditing of the networks; maintain thorough records of who is accessing servers, and modifying, copying, deleting, or downloading files.

- Install software tools—content management, data loss prevention, network forensics—on individual computer workstations to protect files.

- Encrypt data on servers and password-protect company information.

- Incorporate multi-factor authentication measures—biometrics, PINs, and passwords combined with knowledge-based questions—to help verify users of information and computer systems.

- Create a formal corporate policy for mobility—develop measures for centrally controlling and monitoring which devices can be attached to corporate networks and systems and what data can be downloaded, uploaded, and stored on them.

- Formalize a social media policy for the company and implement strategies for minimizing data loss from on-line social networking.

Contingency Planning

- Establish a continuity of operations plan—back up data and systems; create disaster recovery plans; and plan for data breach contingencies.

- Conduct regular penetration testing of company infrastructure as well as of third-party shared service provider systems.

- Establish document creation, retention, and destruction policies.

Resources for Help

- Contact ONCIX or the FBI for assistance in developing effective data protection strategies. If a data breach is suspected, contact the FBI or other law enforcement/organizations for help in identifying and neutralizing the threat.

Page left intentionally blank

Annex B

West and East Accuse China and Russia of Economic Espionage

Other advanced industrial countries principally blame China and Russia for economic espionage that results in large but uncertain monetary costs and job losses. They perceive that China and Russia continue to use traditional human and technical collection methods—particularly against small- and medium-sized businesses—to gather economic information and technologies that save them research and development (R&D) resources and provide entrepreneurial and marketing advantage for their corporate sectors.

- Germany's Federal Office for the Protection of the Constitution (BfV) estimates that German companies lose $28 billion-$71 billion and 30,000-70,000 jobs per year from foreign economic espionage. Approximately 70 percent of all cases involve insiders.

- South Korea says that the costs from foreign economic espionage in 2008 were $82 billion, up from $26 billion in 2004. The South Koreans report that 60 percent of victims are small- and medium-sized businesses and that half of all economic espionage comes from China.[a]

- Japan's Ministry of Economy, Trade, and Industry conducted a survey of 625 manufacturing firms in late 2007 and found that more than 35 percent of those responding reported some form of technology loss. More than 60 percent of those leaks involved China.

France's Renault Affair Highlights Tendency to Blame China

Broad French concerns with Chinese economic espionage formed the background of the hasty—and subsequently retracted—accusations by corporate and political leaders in January 2011 that three top

executives with the Renault automobile company had taken bribes from China in exchange for divulging technology.

- *An investigation by the French internal security service revealed that the accusations against China lacked substance and may have stemmed from a corrupt corporate security officer's attempts to generate investigative work for a friend's consulting business.*

Past Chinese economic espionage against the French automotive industry—including the parts manufacturer Valeo—probably made the French willing to give credence to any accusation of similar malfeasance against China.

Countries acknowledge the growing use of cyber tools for foreign economic collection and espionage and often note difficulties in understanding losses associated with these cyber collection methods. A 2010 survey of 200 industry executives from the power, oil, gas, and water sectors in 12 Western countries, China, and Russia indicates that 85 percent of respondents experienced network intrusions and that government-sponsored sabotage and espionage was the most often cited cyber threat.

- A 2010 Canadian Government report claimed that 86 percent of large Canadian corporations had been hit and that cyber espionage against the private sector had doubled in two years, according to a press report.

- The German BfV offers no reliable figures on the number of cases and amount of damage caused by cyber-enabled economic espionage, adding that their intelligence services are "groping in the dark." The German Government has noted the use of CNE tools and removable media devices, claiming that $99 million are spent annually for IT security.

- UK officials note that the cost of an information security incident averages between $16,000 and $32,000 for a small company and between

---

[a]We have no information on the methodologies that the Germans and South Koreans used to calculate their losses.

$1.6 million and $3.2 million for firms with more than 500 employees. The United Kingdom estimates that attacks on computer systems, including industrial espionage and theft of company trade secrets, cost the private sector $34 billion annually, of which more than 40 percent represents theft of intellectual property such as designs, formulas, and company secrets.

- Germany and South Korea judge that China, in particular, increasingly uses cyber tools to steal trade secrets and achieve plausible deniability, according to press reporting.[b]

- Unidentified CNE operators have accessed more than 150 computers at France's Finance Ministry since late 2010, exfiltrating and redirecting documents relating to the French G-20 presidency to Chinese sites, according to a press report.

- The British Security Service's Center for the Protection of National Infrastructure warned hundreds of UK business leaders in 2010 of Chinese economic espionage practices, including giving gifts of cameras and memory sticks equipped with cyber implants at trade fairs and exhibitions. This followed similar notification sent to 300 UK business leaders in 2007 warning them of a coordinated cyber espionage campaign against the British economy.

- German officials also noted that business travelers' laptops are often stolen during trips to China. The Germans in 2009 highlighted an insider case in which a Chinese citizen downloaded highly sensitive product data from the unidentified German company where he worked to 170 CDs.

China's Response to Allegations of Economic Espionage

China usually responds to public allegations of economic espionage with outright denial and counteraccusations. In 2009 China claimed the Australian mining giant Rio Tinto engaged in six years of espionage activities—bribery and information gathering—that resulted in a loss of iron ore imports for the Chinese steel industry as large

as $107 billion. This loss was more than twice the total profits generated by the Chinese steel industry over that same six-year period, according to the Chinese Government.

Russia also is seen as an important actor in cyber-enabled economic collection and espionage against other countries, albeit a distant second to China. Germany's BfV notes that Russia uses CNE and e-mail interception to save billions of dollars on R&D in the energy, information technology, telecommunications, aerospace, and security sectors.

- The Director-General of the British Security Service publicly stated that Russia, as well as China, is targeting the UK's financial system.

- A Russian automotive company bribed executives at South Korea's GM-Daewoo Auto and Technology to pass thousands of computer files on car engine and component designs in 2009, according to a press report.

- A German insider was convicted of economic espionage in 2008 for passing helicopter technology to the Russian SVR in exchange for $10,000. The insider communicated with his Russian handler through anonymous e-mail addresses.

Countries Suspect Each Other of Committing Economic Espionage

Allies often suspect each other of economic espionage—underlining how countries can be partners in traditional security matters yet competitors in business and trade. Foreign corporate leaders may make accusations that are not publicly endorsed by their governments.

- *According to a 2010 press report, the Germans view France and the United States as the primary perpetrators of economic espionage "among friends."*

- *France's Central Directorate for Domestic Intelligence has called China and the United States the leading "hackers" of French businesses, according to a 2011 press report.*

[b]We lack insight on the processes that the Germans and South Koreans used to attribute cyber activities to China.

Some countries exercise various legislative, intelligence, and diplomatic options to respond to the threat of cyber-enabled economic collection and espionage.

- France and South Korea have proposed new legislation or changes to existing laws to help mitigate the effects of economic espionage. France also is considering a public economic intelligence policy and a classification system for business information.

- France, the United Kingdom, and Australia have issued strategies and revamped bureaucracies to better align resources against cyber and economic espionage threats. France created a 12-person Economic Intelligence Office in 2009 to coordinate French corporate intelligence efforts. The United Kingdom established an Office of Cyber Security to coordinate Whitehall policy under a senior official and a Cyber Security Operations Centre within the Government Communications Headquarters (GCHQ) SIGINT unit. Australia created a cyber espionage branch within its Security Intelligence Organization in 2010.

- The United Kingdom is mobilizing its intelligence services to gather intelligence on potential threats and for operations against economic collection and espionage in cyberspace, according to press reports.

German Espionage Legislation Has Limited Results

Germany's Federal Prosecutor General initiated 31 preliminary proceedings on espionage in 2007, resulting in just one arrest and one conviction. German authorities note that espionage cases are often hindered by diplomatic immunity protections and by attribution issues from operating abroad through cyberspace.

Nearly all countries realize that public and private partnerships are crucial to managing the effects of cyber-enabled economic collection and espionage. The United Kingdom notes that 80 percent of its

critical national infrastructure is owned and operated by the private sector. German authorities would like more corporate feedback and say that most enterprises either do not know when they are victims of cyber espionage or do not want to publicly admit their weaknesses. Most countries engage in some form of corporate outreach.

- The French intelligence services offer regular threat briefings to private companies, according to press reports.

- German authorities regularly exchange information with corporate security officers through a private/public working group that includes Daimler AG, Volkswagen, Porsche, Bayer, the German post office, and the railroad industry.

Corporate Leaders Speak Out on Chinese Espionage

Some foreign corporate executives have singled out Chinese espionage as a threat to their companies.

- *British entrepreneur James Dyson—inventor of the bagless vacuum cleaner—warned in 2011 that Chinese students were stealing technological and scientific secrets from UK universities, according to a press report. He noted that Chinese students were also planting software bugs that would relay information to China even after their departure from the universities.*

- *The CEO of an Australian mining firm said that worries over Chinese and other corporate espionage drove him to adopt a more transparent quarterly pricing mechanism for commodities such as iron ore. He claimed that selling products at market-clearing prices visible to all would minimize the impact of differential information that one party may hold, according to a press article.*

Page left intentionally blank

www.ingramcontent.com/pod-product-compliance
Lightning Source LLC
Chambersburg PA
CBHW060811290526
45792CB00005BA/1616